TaeKwonDo - The Ar

TAEKWONDO
COLORING BOOK

By Alex Man

Breaking Board

SPINNING HOOK KICK

TAEKWONDO

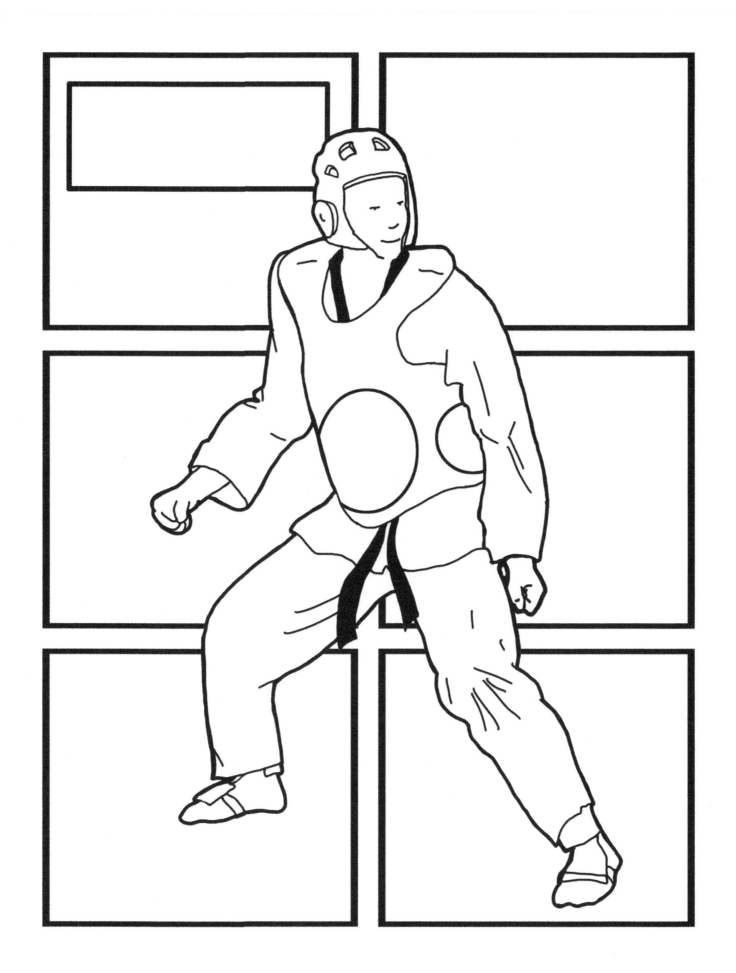

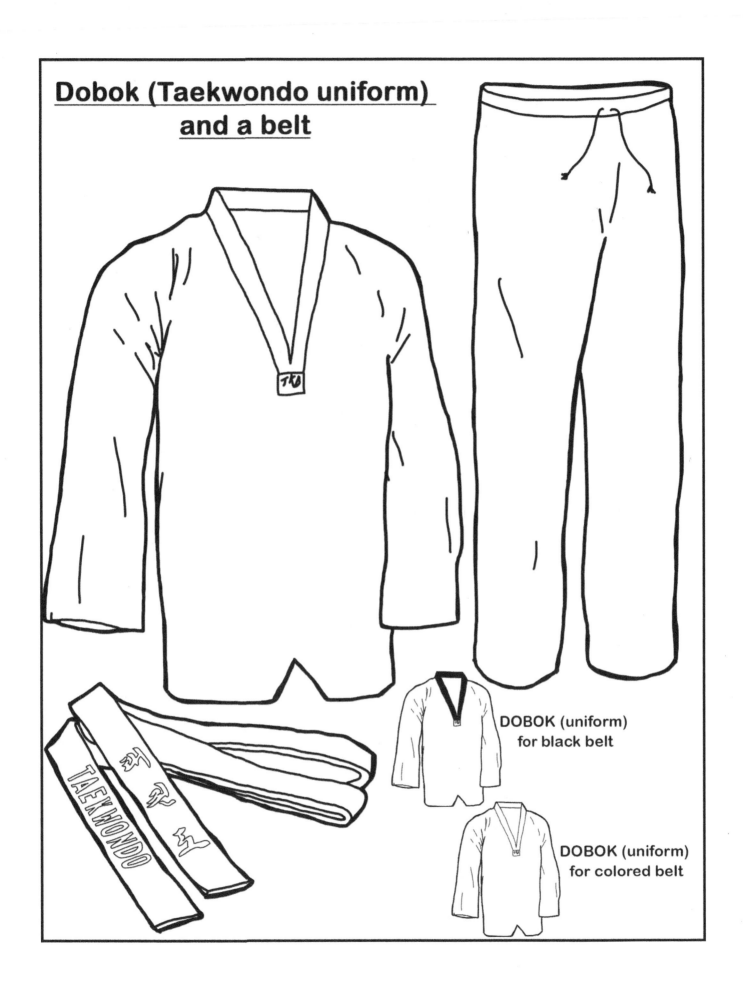

Announcing the winner

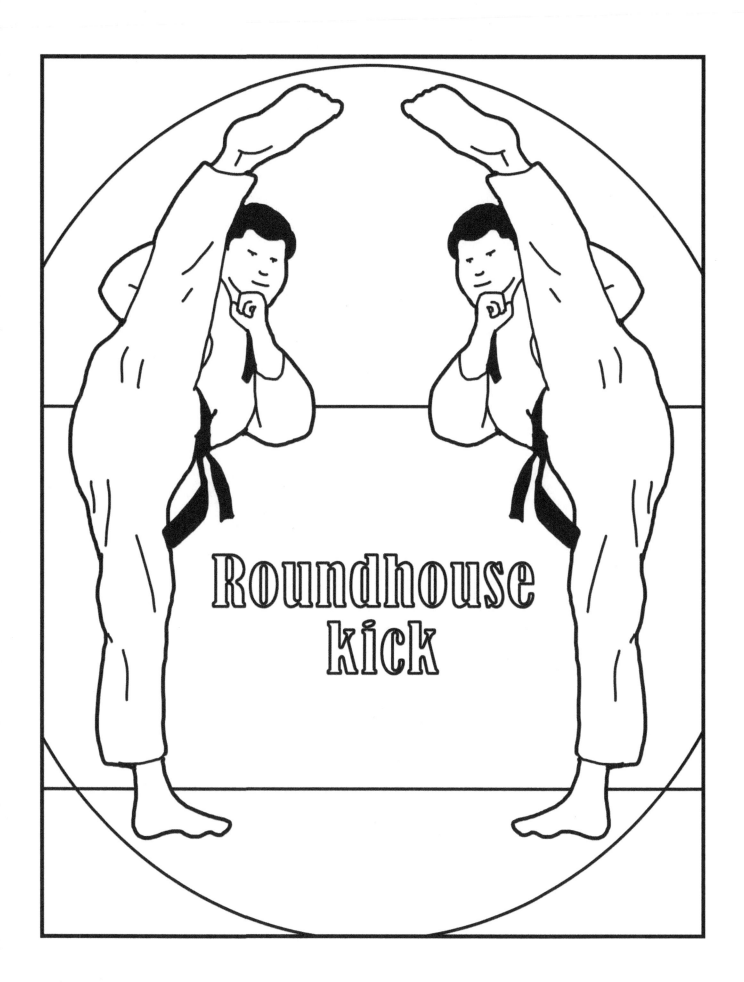

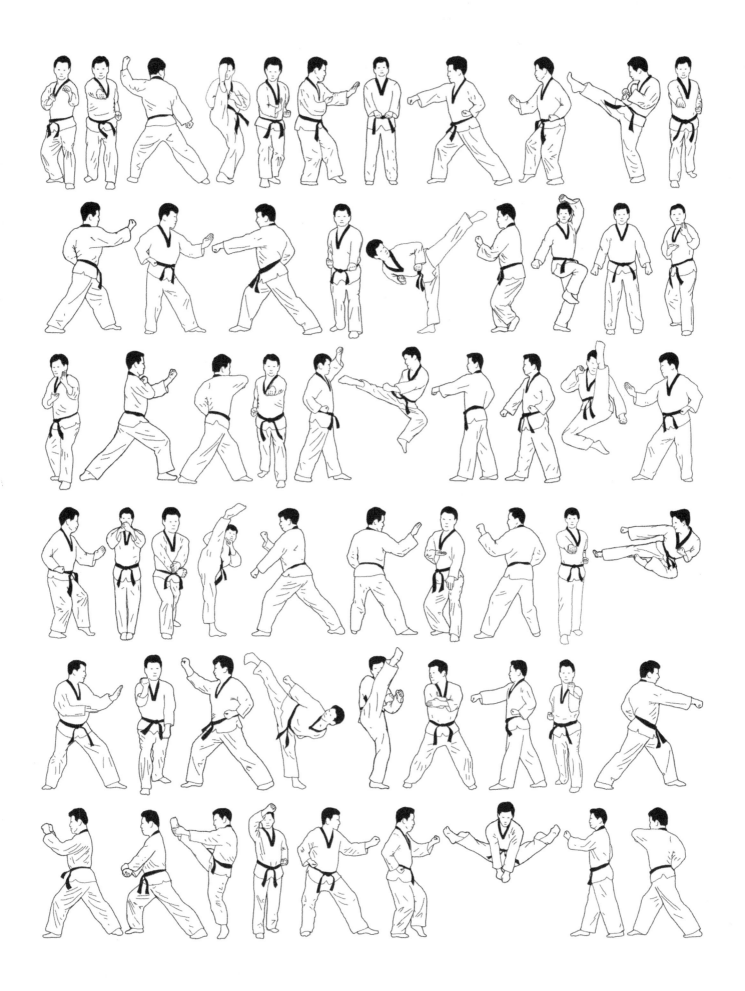

Tiger Stance

Elbow Strike

Tae Kwon Do

Dear reader,
Thank you so much for purchasing my book,
I hope you enjoyed it.
I will appreciate it if you can leave a review on Amazon.
Hope to see you soon.
Keep kicking!
Alex

Copyright 2019 Alex Man

All rights reserved. No part of this publication may be reproduced, distributed, or transmitted in any form or by any means, including photocopying, recording, or other electronic or mechanical methods, without the prior written permission of the author.

Made in the USA
Las Vegas, NV
07 December 2024